Stephen Arterburn
Fred Stoeker with Mike Yorkey

every man's marriage workbook

How to Win Your Wife's Heart...Again and Forever

A Guide for Personal or Group Study

WATERBROOK
PRESS

EVERY MAN'S MARRIAGE WORKBOOK
PUBLISHED BY WATERBROOK PRESS
2375 Telstar Drive, Suite 160
Colorado Springs, Colorado 80920
A division of Random House, Inc.

ISBN 1-57856-678-9

Published in association with the literary agency of Alive Communications, Inc.,
7680 Goddard Street, Suite 200, Colorado Springs, CO 80920.

Printed in the United States of America
2004

10 9 8 7 6 5 4 3 2

contents

questions you may have about this workbook

What will the *Every Man's Marriage Workbook* do for me?

Part of the acclaimed Every Man series, the *Every Man's Marriage Workbook* will help you personalize and apply the groundbreaking principles revealed in the best-selling book *Every Man's Marriage* by Stephen Arterburn and Fred Stoeker with Mike Yorkey. In this workbook you will discover and overcome common misconceptions about exercising biblical authority in the home, learn what every woman most deeply desires in her relationship with a man, and how you can meet this desire and win your wife's heart all over again…and forever. The workbook is designed for either individual or group study.

Is this workbook enough, or do I also need the book *Every Man's Marriage?*

Included in each weekly study you'll find a number of excerpts from *Every Man's Marriage,* each marked at the beginning and the end by this symbol: 📖. Nevertheless, the most beneficial approach is to also read *Every Man's Marriage* as you go through this companion workbook. You'll find the appropriate chapters to read listed at the beginning of each weekly study.

The lessons look long. Do I need to work through each one?

This workbook is designed to guide your exploration of all the material, but you may find it best to focus your time and discussion on some sections and questions more than others.

To help your pacing, we've designed the workbook so it can most easily be used in either an eight-week or a twelve-week program.

- *For the eight-week track,* simply follow the basic organization of the eight different weekly lessons.
- *For the twelve-week track,* the lessons marked for Weeks Two, Five, Six, and Seven can be divided into two parts (you'll see the dividing place marked in the text).

(In addition, of course, you may decide on an even slower pace, whether you're going through the workbook individually or in a group.)

Above all, keep in mind that the purpose of the workbook is to assist you in specific applications of the biblical truths taught in *Every Man's Marriage.* The wide array of questions included in each weekly study is meant to help you approach this practical application from different angles, with personal reflection and self-examination. Allowing adequate time to prayerfully reflect on each question will be much more valuable to you than rushing through the workbook.

How do I bring together a small group to go through this workbook?

You'll get far more out of this workbook if you're able to work through it with a small group of like-minded men. And what do you do if you don't know of a group that's going through the workbook? Start such a group of your own!

If you take a copy of the book *Every Man's Marriage,* plus a copy of this companion workbook, and show them to other Christian men, you'll be surprised at how many will indicate an interest in joining you to explore this topic together. And it doesn't require a long commitment from them. The workbook is set up so you can complete one lesson per week and finish in only eight weeks—or if you'd like to proceed at a slower pace, you can follow the instructions provided for covering the content in a twelve-week track.

Your once-a-week meeting could be scheduled during a lunch hour, in the early morning before work begins, on a weekday evening, or even on Saturday morning. The meeting place can be an office or meeting room at work, a room at a club or restaurant, a classroom at church, or someone's basement or den at home. Choose a place where your discussion won't be overheard by others, so everyone will be comfortable sharing candidly and freely.

This workbook follows a simple, easy-to-use format. First, each man completes a week's lesson on his own. Then, when you come together that week, you discuss together the group questions provided under the Every Man's TALK heading in each week's lesson. Of course, if you have time, you can also discuss at length any of the other questions or topics in the lesson; we guarantee the men in your group will find these to be worth exploring. And they're likely as well to have plenty of their own questions to add to the discussion.

It's best if one person in your group is designated as the facilitator. This person is not a lecturer or teacher, but he simply has the responsibility to keep the discussion moving and to ensure that each man in the group has an opportunity to join in.

At the beginning, remind the men of the simple ground rule that anything shared in the group stays in the group—everything's confidential. This will help the men feel safer about sharing honestly and openly in an environment of trust.

Finally, we encourage you during each meeting to allow time for prayer—conversational, short-sentence prayers expressed honestly before God. Many men don't feel comfortable praying aloud in front of others, so in an understanding way, do all you can to help them overcome that barrier.

Note: Because *Every Man's Marriage* is based in large part on Fred Stoeker's personal story, the first-person accounts excerpted for this workbook are Fred's unless otherwise indicated.

when love grows cold

This week's reading assignment:

The introduction and chapters 1–3 in *Every Man's Marriage*

I sat across the kitchen table from my wife, Brenda, and I could tell she was waiting until she had my undivided attention.

Then she looked intently into my eyes and changed my world. "I don't know how else to say this to you, so I'll say it straight," she began. "My feelings for you are dead."

Her words arrived like a fastball pitch to the solar plexus. Dead? My head spun. Where was this coming from? How could I have messed things up so badly that my wife—the love of my life—now felt totally numb to me?

—from chapter 1 in *Every Man's Marriage*

📖 EVERY MAN'S TRUTH
(Your Personal Journey into God's Word)

As you begin this first study, take some time to read and meditate upon the Bible passages below, which have to do with the deep and abiding love that God has for you and your wife. Keep in mind that this love is unconditional and that it's a power greater than any problem you may be facing. Let that love wash over you each day. Let it motivate you to respond with thankfulness.

Give thanks to the LORD, for he is good;
    his love endures forever.

…for he satisfies the thirsty
    and fills the hungry with good things. (Psalm 107:1,9)

"Therefore I am now going to allure her;
    I will lead her into the desert
    and speak tenderly to her.
There I will give her back her vineyards,
    and will make the Valley of Achor a door of hope.
There she will sing as in the days of her youth,
    as in the day she came up out of Egypt.

"In that day," declares the LORD,
    "you will call me 'my husband';
    you will no longer call me 'my master.'
I will remove the names of the Baals from her lips;
    no longer will their names be invoked.…
I will betroth you in faithfulness,
    and you will acknowledge the LORD.

"In that day I will respond,"
    declares the LORD—
"I will respond to the skies,
    and they will respond to the earth;
and the earth will respond to the grain,
    the new wine and oil,
    and they will respond to Jezreel.

I will plant her for myself in the land;
  I will show my love to the one I called
    'Not my loved one.'
I will say to those called 'Not my people,'
    'You are my people';
  and they will say, 'You are my God.' "
    (Hosea 2:14-17,20-23)

What, then, shall we say in response to this? If God is for us, who can be against us?... Who shall separate us from the love of Christ? Shall trouble or hardship or persecution or famine or nakedness or danger or sword? As it is written:

> "For your sake we face death all day long; we are considered as sheep to be slaughtered."

No, in all these things we are more than conquerors through him who loved us. For I am convinced that neither death nor life, neither angels nor demons, neither the present nor the future, nor any powers, neither height nor depth, nor anything else in all creation, will be able to separate us from the love of God that is in Christ Jesus our Lord. (Romans 8:31,35-39)

1. Focus on Psalm 107:9. In what ways are you thirsty and hungry these days? How could God's love become more satisfying for you in your everyday life?

2. In Hosea, God pictures His love for Israel in terms of a husband loving a wayward wife. In effect, we, God's people, are that wife. How
   does God's love feel to you right now?

3. Have you ever felt separated from God's love? What encouragement
   can you draw from Paul's words about this?

4. For what aspects of God's love in your life are you particularly thankful? Take some moments to recall that love and to express your grati-
   tude directly to the Lord right now.

☑️ EVERY MAN's CHOICE
(Questions for Personal Reflection and Examination)

📖 In the early days, my heart skipped a beat every time I saw Brenda walk across a room. Not anymore. More often than not, our evenings ended the same way: After hitting the light on the nightstand, I'd settle my head into my pillow, only to hear these sickening words in the darkness: "Fred, we have something to talk about." 📖

📖 Our communication patterns changed that day. I had once been blind, but now I could see. Over the next days and weeks, I listened closely when I asked her, "What exactly have I done? How did I kill your feelings?"

I found that we hadn't been locked in a simple conflict of wills at all. I had been trampling her to the depths of her soul. To rectify the matter, I had to discover the role of "male submission" in marriage. But first, of course, the trampling had to stop. 📖

5. Recall the early days in your relationship with your wife. What feelings from those days could you realistically hope to regain in the future?

6. If your wife were to say: "We have something to talk about," what would be the top three items on her list? Why?

7. What does the idea of trampling mean to you? In what ways do you think you may have been guilty of this in the past? Do you agree that discovering the role of male submission could help?

📖 EVERY MAN'S WALK

(Your Guide to Personal Application)

> 📖 I shut the door and stared for a long time at the refrigerator through tear-filled eyes. Then I pointed to heaven, declaring, "God, I don't care how much gravel I have to eat, but I am not getting a divorce."
>
> That's how desperate I was. I'd eat rocks if that would save my marriage. I knew it was time to pay a real price, a much deeper price. God said in Ephesians 5 that I must lay down my life for my marriage, just as He laid down His life for His bride, the church. I hadn't even approached such sacrificial love. 📖

> 📖 If I learned anything in that Sunday school class for couples, it was that men are primarily responsible to complete God's call to marital oneness (drawn especially from Ephesians 5:23, where we're told, "For the husband is the head of the wife as Christ is the head of the church, his body, of which he is the Savior"). While women have clear responsibilities in a marriage, let's speak plainly: Who is God likely to hold most responsible?... I knew marriage and my love

for Brenda was my highest calling. It was time to step up and make a deeper commitment, but I was clueless and running out of time. To resurrect my marriage, I was willing to take drastic action at any cost, even if that meant bringing in a third party. 📖

📖 Regardless of whether Scripture is involved, any stumbling block we place in the way of oneness with our wives is sin. It weakens God's purpose for marriage and flaunts our leadership at the expense of God's work. 📖

8. Are you as committed to avoiding divorce as Fred was? What, specifically, would "eating gravel" mean for you?

9. In your mind, what are the pros and cons of seeking a third party's help? How willing are you to try this? Why?

10. List a few of the ways you could fulfill your responsibility to complete marital oneness. Be as practical as possible.

11. What are some of the stumbling blocks you may have placed in the way of oneness in the past? What are some of your ideas for removing these? How could you approach your wife in order to talk about this during the week ahead?

12. In quiet, review what you have written and learned in this week's study. If further thoughts or prayer requests come to your mind and heart, you may want to write them here.

13. a) What for you was the most meaningful concept or truth in this week's study?

 b) How would you talk this over with God? Write your response here as a prayer to Him.

c) What do you believe God wants you to do in response to this week's study?

👨👩 EVERY MAN'S TALK

(Constructive Topics and Questions for Group Discussion)

Key Highlights from the Book for Reading Aloud and Discussing

📖 I had trampled Brenda, crushing the opportunity for oneness in our marriage. I had stampeded her concerns, stepped on her feelings. Such trampling is sinning against your wife.

Yes, I said *sinning*. If you're thinking I'm off the wall and you're ready to put this book down, don't move so fast. Most of us Christian men sin against our wives regularly, but we're just too blind to see it. Odds are, you're a bit blind too. So why do I say *trampling* instead of *sinning*?

The word *sin* has lost its communication value in our culture partly because it's considered too judgmental. No one likes to be called a sinner. *That's for people who are really bad.* 📖

📖 There were some things I (Steve) could do immediately to become the husband Sandy had always desired. I limited my travel to two days per week. I came home from work by 6 P.M. and left my briefcase at the office so I wouldn't work at home. I regularly called Sandy to ask her to join me for lunch. Most of all, I decided to meet her needs by lavishing thoughtful gifts and getaway weekends on her—and by taking the trash out without being asked and by making sure my dirty laundry actually reached the clothes hamper and then by learning how to operate the washing machine. 📖

📖 Smart husbands always ask: Would I rather be right or righteous? 📖

Discussion Questions

A. Which parts of these chapters were most helpful or encouraging to you? Why?

p2 4

B. Name some of the common trampling behaviors of husbands (while remaining anonymous!). Why is it so easy for us to sin this way? *Eph 5:22 ⇒ :25*

B₂ What happens when we assert our authority *Mitigation Eph 5:25 1 Pet 3:7*

C. What is your reaction to the things Steve found to do for his wife? Do they seem trivial or important to you? How do you think your own wife would react if you tried something similar in the coming week?

p 31

D. In your opinion, what does Fred mean by contrasting being right and being righteous? Offer a practical example that shows the difference.

E. If you were to commit to taking the first small step toward warming up the love in your marriage, what would you do? How can the other men in your group pray for you right now?

starting to breathe again

This week's reading assignment:

chapters 4–7 in *Every Man's Marriage*

The Bible uses the terms daughter *and* ewe lamb *to capture a heavenly message. Just as Bathsheba was precious to Uriah, your wife is precious to you. She lives with you and lies in your arms. She's to be treated according to her value to God as a child created in His image. You've been entrusted with the priceless essence of another human soul, so precious to God that He paid dearly for her with the death of His own Son.*

—from chapter 4 in *Every Man's Marriage*

EVERY MAN'S TRUTH
(Your Personal Journey into God's Word)

The Bible passages below continue with the theme of God's great love for us. This comes through in Jesus' statements about the heavenly Father's concern for the physical welfare of His creatures. Then the apostle Paul, in one of the most glorious statements in the New Testament, lays out the spiritual blessings of salvation that flow to us through God's pure grace. As you consider these biblical messages, ask the Holy Spirit to lead you into specific, practical applications for your daily life.

Therefore I tell you, do not worry about your life, what you will eat or drink; or about your body, what you will wear. Is not life more important than food, and the body more important than clothes? Look at the birds of the air; they do not sow or reap or store away in barns, and yet your heavenly Father feeds them. Are you not much more valuable than they? Who of you by worrying can add a single hour to his life?

And why do you worry about clothes? See how the lilies of the field grow. They do not labor or spin. Yet I tell you that not even Solomon in all his splendor was dressed like one of these. If that is how God clothes the grass of the field, which is here today and tomorrow is thrown into the fire, will he not much more clothe you, O you of little faith? (Matthew 6:25-30)

Praise be to the God and Father of our Lord Jesus Christ, who has blessed us in the heavenly realms with every spiritual blessing in Christ. For he chose us in him before the creation of the world to be holy and blameless in his sight. In love he predestined us to be adopted as his sons through Jesus Christ, in accordance with his pleasure and will—to the praise of his glorious grace, which he has freely given us in the One he loves. In him we have redemption through his blood, the forgiveness of sins, in accordance with the riches of God's grace that he lavished on us with all wisdom and understanding. And he made known to us the mystery of his will according to his good pleasure, which he purposed in Christ, to be put into effect when the times will have reached their fulfillment—to bring all things in heaven and on earth together under one head, even Christ.

In him we were also chosen, having been predestined
according to the plan of him who works out everything in
conformity with the purpose of his will, in order that we,
who were the first to hope in Christ, might be for the praise
of his glory. (Ephesians 1:3-12)

1. The Bible passages above speak of God's loving care for us physically
   and spiritually. Make a list of some of the specific blessings God has
   provided in your life over the years. Take some time to offer thanks.

2. What types of needs are most pressing in your life these days—
   physical care from God or spiritual renewal from God? Why?

3. Jesus spoke of God's concern for even the smallest details of our needs.
   How much do you think He cares about your marriage? What are
   some of the small and large issues you would like God to care for in
   this relationship?

4. The apostle Paul said that we have been adopted as sons of the Father. How does this make you feel? Consider: What are some of the implications of this sonship for practical daily living? for how you will act as a husband?

5. Since you have complete forgiveness and acceptance from God, are you able to extend this kind of grace toward your wife? What changes will be required in you if you are to do a better job of this?

☑ EVERY MAN'S CHOICE
(Questions for Personal Reflection and Examination)

> 📖 I came to the stunning realization that the Lord Himself created Brenda and loves her very essence.... Earlier in our marriage, I hadn't seen Brenda in this light. Truth be told, there were times when I viewed her as a stubborn old goat or, worse, a mule. I never saw her as a precious ewe lamb.... I suspected that I'd been trampling Brenda's essence for a long time. 📖

📖 Your wife is aching to be one with you. The whole plan of marriage was designed that you might be one with her. And because women were created for relationship, her highest priority is that you would honor her essence as you do your own, living in mutual submission with her. This is every woman's desire. 📖

6. How do you view your wife these days? How has your view changed over the years? What are some of the causes for this change?

7. What evidence have you seen that your wife aches for oneness with you? How have you typically responded? In the most practical terms, what would it mean for you to honor your wife's essence?

 EVERY MAN'S WALK
(Your Guide to Personal Application)

📖 I'm commanded by Scripture to love Brenda as Christ loved the church. How did Christ love the church? In perfect kindness: "A bruised reed he will not break, and a smoldering wick he will not snuff out" (Matthew 12:20). Christ doesn't trample us in our weaknesses. But I trampled Brenda. 📖

📖 There's nothing emotional or mystical about the command to love our wives as ourselves. If Rick came home an hour earlier, he'd be loving her as himself and making room for her essence.... It's all about action; it's all about loving sacrifice. 📖

8. Give a practical example of what a husband's kindness should look like in a marriage relationship.

9. What does trampling look like in your marriage? When are you most likely to succumb to it?

10. Review the candy cane illustration. How would you describe the ratio of colors on your own marital candy cane? Make a short list of ways you could begin to make the colors more evenly intertwined.

11. Why is oneness more about action than emotion? Think about the implications of this for your own relationship with your wife. What action do you need to take during the coming week?

12. In quiet, review what you have written and learned in this week's study. If further thoughts or prayer requests come to your mind and heart, you may want to write them here.

13. a) What for you was the most meaningful concept or truth in chapters 4 and 5?

    b) How would you talk this over with God? Write your response here as a prayer to Him.

c) What do you believe God wants you to do in response to this
week's study?

EVERY MAN'S TALK

(Constructive Topics and Questions for Group Discussion)

Key Highlights from the Book for Reading Aloud and Discussing

📖 Jesus taught us submission to oneness by example. He
laid down His life in full submission for the sake of our relationship with Him, though we were yet sinners. Only then
did He ask in return our full submission to His authority.
His submission to oneness and our submission to His
authority made oneness possible.... Mutual submission is
God's will for Christian relationships: "Submit to one
another out of reverence for Christ" (Ephesians 5:21). 📖

p. 58 📖 The beauty of her home was a deep part of Bernice's
soul essence. Her husband needn't *enjoy* hanging wallpaper.
He just had to *do* it. And if he couldn't do it, then he
needed to hire someone who could. He needn't develop
the same emotional attachment to their home as Bernice
experienced, but he did need to exert himself in the same
manner that he did for his own projects. This is male
submission to oneness. 📖

PS 59

📖 Most of us husbands aren't thinking about what our wives truly desire. Our wives want rich communication and a bond that no one can touch. They long to blossom in marriage. They long for our eyes to meet in meaningful dialogue. 📖

Pg 59

Discussion Questions

A. Which parts of these chapters were most helpful or encouraging to you? Why? — *Pg 59* — *Restaurant → older couples*

B. Give your definition of *mutual submission* by illustrating it with a practical example from your marriage.

C. Review the story of Bernice, Stan, and the bathroom project. Talk about how Bernice was feeling. Why do you think Stan delayed the project for so long? How are you like, or unlike, Stan?

D. Do you agree that husbands usually aren't thinking about their wives' desires? Explain.

E. In spite of our differences, how are we in tune with our wives when it comes to wanting oneness? How can we express this in ways our wives can understand? What changes in approach might we need to try?

For a twelve-week study,
save the following material for next week.

☑ EVERY MAN'S CHOICE

(Questions for Personal Reflection and Examination)

> 📖 I certainly didn't see the train coming my direction.
> Brenda and I never fought before the wedding, and we
> even liked the same pizza—Canadian bacon and pineapple.
> Surely our marriage was a match made in heaven. Yet on
> one lovely September evening the chiming of wedding bells
> faded quickly in the din of a terrible row between us. 📖

> 📖 All too often, any "sacrifice" we make for our wives is
> more about burnishing our own images than actually doing
> something for our wives. 📖

14. How did you know your marriage was a match made in heaven? What were your first clues that there might be trouble in paradise?

15. Think of some of the ways you've sacrificed for your wife in the past. Which were genuine sacrifices, without thought of your own image (as in Fred's car-warming story)? Which instances were less genuine? Why?

 Every Man's WALK
(Your Guide to Personal Application)

> 📖 Role models aside, what about you? Do you have blind spots as a result of these ten ["love chiller"] traits? How would you know? Someone has to tell you.… So I asked four men this question: "What traits or characteristics do you see in me that would keep me from becoming an effective leader in this church?" 📖

> 📖 *But Fred and Steve, my wife is not my master!* True, but becoming-one-with-her-essence is your master. You submit your rights in whatever way necessary as leader to attain this, not because she has authority over you, but because you love her. You've been commanded to love her in precisely this way by someone who *does* have authority over you—Jesus Christ. 📖

16. Would you have the courage to ask another man (or men) about your blind spots? If so, begin making some plans to contact one or more men about this, following Fred's example. Consider: What are your hunches about some of the things they might say?

17. Spend some time reflecting on the ten love chillers that were discussed in chapter 6. Evaluate your own tendencies under each of the

headings. Make a note about a way you could improve in at least three of the areas.

18. In quiet, review what you have written and learned in this week's study. If further thoughts or prayer requests come to your mind and heart, you may want to write them here.

19. a) What for you was the most meaningful concept or truth in chapters 6 and 7?

b) How would you talk this over with God? Write your response here as a prayer to Him.

c) What do you believe God wants you to do in response to this week's study?

👤👤 Every Man's TALK
(Constructive Topics and Questions for Group Discussion)

Key Highlights from the Book for Reading Aloud and Discussing

📖 You probably have a few stories of your own to tell from your early days of marriage. 📖

📖 We men are just different from women—and there are some qualities about us and how we relate to women and marriage that we definitely need to understand and confront. We might call these characteristics potential "love chillers" in a marriage because they tend to induce a cooling effect on the flow of warmth and affection in the relationship. 📖

📖 Servant leadership is more than washing your wife's feet once in a while or vacuuming before she returns home from a trip to the mall. It's more than washing dishes, running a load of laundry, or filling her car with gas. We have neighbors who would do these things for us in a pinch. Serving isn't something we *do*—it's something we *are*. 📖

Discussion Questions

F. Spend some time telling some (humorous) stories about your early days in marriage. (Be careful not to overshare or put down your wife in any way! Just have some lighthearted fun for a few minutes.)

G. Talk through the ten love chillers presented in chapter 6. Which one or two of these seemed to strike home most powerfully to you? Why? What can you do to improve in these areas?

H. Why is it so important to maintain the distinction between leadership as doing and leadership as being? What are the practical implications of this in your own marriage?

I. Be sure to include items from the responses to *G* above in your prayer time together.

manifesting your bondservant heart (part A)

This week's reading assignment:

chapters 8–10 in *Every Man's Marriage*.

A bondservant is always at his master's call. That's fine with him. He lives to love and serve his master anyway. He never says, "I think I'll take a night off." His time is never his own, unless his master says so.

—from chapter 9 in *Every Man's Marriage*

EVERY MAN'S TRUTH
(Your Personal Journey into God's Word)

Read and meditate upon the Bible passages below, which deal with God's sacrificial love—and our loving response. Consider once again how deeply you are loved. Think about the sense in which God "humbles" Himself to love us. Then think about how this soul-nurturing truth can move you to love your wife in a self-sacrificing way.

When I consider your heavens,

    the work of your fingers,

the moon and the stars,

    which you have set in place,

what is man that you are mindful of him,

    the son of man that you care for him?

You made him a little lower than the heavenly beings

    and crowned him with glory and honor.

        (Psalm 8:3-5)

Your attitude should be the same as that of Christ Jesus:

Who, being in very nature God,

    did not consider equality with God something

        to be grasped,

but made himself nothing,

    taking the very nature of a servant,

    being made in human likeness.

And being found in appearance as a man,

    he humbled himself

    and became obedient to death—even death on a cross!

Therefore God exalted him to the highest place

    and gave him the name that is above every name,

that at the name of Jesus every knee should bow,

    in heaven and on earth and under the earth,

and every tongue confess that Jesus Christ is Lord,

    to the glory of God the Father.

        (Philippians 2:5-11)

If I give all I possess to the poor and surrender my body to the flames, but have not love, I gain nothing.

Love is patient, love is kind. It does not envy, it does not boast, it is not proud. It is not rude, it is not self-seeking, it is not easily angered, it keeps no record of wrongs. Love does not delight in evil but rejoices with the truth. It always protects, always trusts, always hopes, always perseveres.

Love never fails. (1 Corinthians 13:3-8)

1. Why is the psalmist so amazed? What unexpected aspect of God's personality comes through here? What is your reaction?

2. Jesus willingly laid down His life as a servant, though He is Lord of all. Is this a realistic example for us to follow? How?

3. Having humbled Himself, Jesus was then exalted. Do you see this as a common pattern in life? Can you think of ways this pattern might unfold in a marriage?

4. Review the characteristics of love, as taught by the apostle Paul. Which qualities do you most appreciate in God's approach to you? Which do you most desire in your approach to your wife?

☑ EVERY MAN'S CHOICE
(Questions for Personal Reflection and Examination)

📖 You have few rights of your own besides those granted by the "master." Understanding this ensures that [your wife's] convictions and essence are considered in decisions. When you go through married life saying, "I have a right to _____," it doesn't matter what you pencil in.... But these aren't rights until your wife agrees they are. 📖

📖 Let's reason this out for a minute. No master purchased a slave hoping this servant would make it more difficult for him to express his gifts and ministries. And no bond-servant ever laid his earlobe to the post in a desire to make things tougher for the master. He loved his master, and he gave up everything to ensure his master could fully live, to ensure his gifts and ministries could fully blossom. What about your wife? Are you making it easy for her to please God? 📖

5. How do you react to the idea that "you have few rights of your own"?

6. If you were to fill in the blank in the first quote with some of your rights, which ones would you be in agreement about with your wife? Which would you disagree about? Why?

7. Think about your wife's gifts for service and ministry. How could you make it easier for her to use these gifts in order to please God?

Every Man's WALK
(Your Guide to Personal Application)

> In the end, no matter how I looked at it, I came to this conclusion: Brenda needed me more than I needed softball. I knew she desired that I stay home with her rather than do

bat cleanup. Under these circumstances, her desire was more important than mine. 📖

📖 Most of us learn pretty quickly that we must check with our wives before planning our schedules. Cheryl says, "I appreciate how Dave always checks with me before committing evenings or weekend time with a friend." That's great, and it should be normal, everyday behavior. 📖

8. For Fred, it was softball. What is it for you?

9. How can a guy say "her desire [is] more important than mine" without succumbing to bitterness or resentment? How would you handle this?

10. List some of the areas where your desires and your wife's seem to conflict. Think about which of these areas of conflict require a change of attitude in you. Which simply require a change in scheduling?

11. What are some of the practical steps you could take to do a better job of scheduling? For example: hanging a family calendar in a prominent place. Your ideas?

12. In quiet, review what you have written and learned in this week's study. If further thoughts or prayer requests come to your mind and heart, you may want to write them here.

13. a) What for you was the most meaningful concept or truth in this week's study?

   b) How would you talk this over with God? Write your response here as a prayer to Him.

c) What do you believe God wants you to do in response to this week's study?

Every Man's TALK

(Constructive Topics and Questions for Group Discussion)

Key Highlights from the Book for Reading Aloud and Discussing

📖 What I'm trying to say is that the "master" defines your rights. (Remember that though we refer to your wife as your "master," it's shorthand for the fact that becoming-one-with-her-essence is your God-given master.). Why? Because you're called to oneness, and her essence sets the terms. Defending your rights is not conducive to even *seeing* your wife's convictions and essence, let alone honoring them. 📖

📖 If you're married to a wilting or warring woman, you might want to consider how much time, and what kind of time, you're giving her. In other words, what's your own approach to time in marriage? 📖

📖 Such a simple thing like going over to my neighbor's on Brenda's behest seemed to speak volumes to her heart. Sure, I'd been right all along. If there were ever a job for Chief Tiebreaker, this was it.... But would I have been righteous? I would have shut down her voice before I'd heard that urgency in her heart, burying her ministry. 📖

Discussion Questions

A. Which parts of these chapters were most helpful or encouraging to you? Why?

B. What is your current understanding of becoming-one-with-her-essence? How would you illustrate it in a practical way?

C. When have you experienced your master's defining your rights? Talk about how this was for you.

D. Are you married to a wilting or warring woman? Discuss how husbands of each of these should approach time and scheduling in marriage.

E. Recall Fred's story about going over to visit his neighbor when Brenda asked him to do so. Put yourself in the story, as Fred, and retell it! How would the ending be similar or different? (Try to be as candid and honest as possible in conveying your likely reactions in this situation.)

F. Fred felt as if he'd earned the right to some relaxation. Do you feel the same way? What is your level of irritation when your wife tries to interfere with this "right"? What are your prospects for change in this area?

G. How do you define quality time? Offer a personal example.

H. As you close your group time together, ask for prayer requests related to the challenges of manifesting a bondservant heart in marriage. (Be sure to guard the privacy of each man's marital relationship while dealing with genuine needs.)

manifesting your bondservant heart (part B)

This week's reading assignment:

chapters 11–13 in *Every Man's Marriage*.

God wants marriage to be a transforming agent in your life, and you need to embrace that divine purpose. He wants marriage to grind away your rough edges, and He chose your wife—this particular package, with just these flaws—because she was best suited for this job in you. She'll force you to grow up, so that you will learn to love when you don't feel like loving.

—from chapter 11 in *Every Man's Marriage*

EVERY MAN'S TRUTH
(Your Personal Journey into God's Word)

In the first three weeks you studied Bible passages dealing with the Father's love for you. Now turn to some scriptures that convey the Son's example of servanthood. Remember that marriage is a reflection of the relationship between Christ and us (His church). That relationship flourishes amid humility and a spirit of self-giving. This is the kind of leadership Jesus pursues with us. He leads by example, not by power or coercion. He gently invites us to follow by continuing to serve, no matter what our response.

> He was despised and rejected by men,
>   a man of sorrows, and familiar with suffering.
> Like one from whom men hide their faces
>   he was despised, and we esteemed him not.
>
> Surely he took up our infirmities
>   and carried our sorrows,
> yet we considered him stricken by God,
>   smitten by him, and afflicted.
> But he was pierced for our transgressions,
>   he was crushed for our iniquities;
> the punishment that brought us peace was upon him,
>   and by his wounds we are healed.
> We all, like sheep, have gone astray,
>   each of us has turned to his own way;
> and the LORD has laid on him
>   the iniquity of us all.
>
> He was oppressed and afflicted,
>   yet he did not open his mouth;
> he was led like a lamb to the slaughter,
>   and as a sheep before her shearers is silent,
>   so he did not open his mouth.
>   (Isaiah 53:3-7)

Jesus knew that the Father had put all things under his
power, and that he had come from God and was returning
to God; so he got up from the meal, took off his outer
clothing, and wrapped a towel around his waist. After
that, he poured water into a basin and began to wash his
disciples' feet, drying them with the towel that was wrapped
around him.

He came to Simon Peter, who said to him, "Lord, are you
going to wash my feet?"

Jesus replied, "You do not realize now what I am doing,
but later you will understand....

"Now that I, your Lord and Teacher, have washed your
feet, you also should wash one another's feet. I have set you
an example that you should do as I have done for you."
(John 13:3-7,14-15)

My command is this: Love each other as I have loved you.
Greater love has no one than this, that he lay down his life
for his friends. (John 15:12-13)

1. Isaiah writes of the Messiah as a suffering servant. What qualities of
   heart would be required to fulfill such a role? In your opinion, why
   was it important for the prophet to stress that the servant "did not
   open his mouth"?

2. Consider the reasons Peter would be so amazed at Jesus' servant actions. How easy or difficult is it for you to see yourself in the servant role in marriage?

3. When have you, in effect, laid down your life for a friend? What were the inner challenges and obstacles you had to overcome to do this?

4. What are the similarities and differences between the servant love of Christ for you and your love for your wife? What key insight do you gain from these scriptures?

☑ EVERY MAN'S CHOICE
(Questions for Personal Reflection and Examination)

📖 When I (Steve) married Sandy, I couldn't believe all the stuff I hadn't known about her earlier. I started seeing all these things I didn't like, things that made me feel uncomfortable. I embarked on a mission to change her so I could have the freedom to be me. Actually, what I was looking for was an excuse not to grow. Over time I discovered something you can discover also: *The things that irritated me the most were the things God was using to transform me....* Everything in Sandy that was different from me was God's challenging me to grow. 📖

📖 Have you chosen to draw your prestige primarily from your relationship with your wife? Probably not. Truth be told, most of us draw our prestige from our careers. It's our work and what we do five days a week (or more!) that lifts our self-esteem, not whom we're married to. If you must work long hours and nights for six weeks, it may mean some unusual business project came up. Everyone can understand that. But if you work long hours and nights for six months, then you've made a crucial decision about what you value most in life. 📖

5. Have you ever considered that your wife's weaknesses could be used by God for your spiritual growth? If this is true, which "irritations" do you need to pay more attention to—as heavenly messages?

6. From what part of life do you draw your greatest sense of prestige? Explain why.

7. Make a short list of your most cherished values. Where do marriage and family come in? How obvious would your priorities be to an outside observer?

 EVERY MAN'S **WALK**

(Your Guide to Personal Application)

📖 Are you allowing for your "master's" weakness, loving your wife for who she is *this day*—not for who she might be at some other future date down the line? Sure, you may be shocked and dismayed at the weaknesses in your wife that were hidden until this life spun you both in its new direction. Still, your spouse has a heart that beats like a little lamb's heart, a heart that still skips through meadows of hope and desire, longing for your love. This part of her may be difficult to see. 📖

📖 Since our wives have gifts we don't have, releasing their voice in our homes can bring incredible blessings. Case in point: Melissa and Kevin's [story].... It's especially critical to hear your wife's voice when she's speaking from the very center of her gifts. Our wives are fellow heirs of grace, every bit as worthy to lead our homes as we are, except for God's grace in granting us that role. This ability to lead is especially evident in the areas of their strengths. 📖

8. List some of your major weaknesses. Then list some of your wife's weaknesses. How accepting are you of the items on each list?

9. Can you accept your wife for what she is right now? If not, what would it take for you to let go of your vision for what your wife could be in the future? How do you think this transformation (in you) would affect your marriage relationship?

10. What does it mean to release your wife's voice? In what ways does she need to be heard? What can you do to help this happen?

11. Recall the story of Melissa and Kevin in chapter 12. How do you think it benefited Kevin to let Melissa's voice and leadership come through? In light of their experience, what general principle can you formulate for yourself?

12. In quiet, review what you have written and learned in this week's study. If further thoughts or prayer requests come to your mind and heart, you may want to write them here.

13. a) What for you was the most meaningful concept or truth in this week's study?

b) How would you talk this over with God? Write your response here as a prayer to Him.

c) What do you believe God wants you to do in response to this week's study?

👥 Every Man's TALK

(Constructive Topics and Questions for Group Discussion)

Key Highlights from the Book for Reading Aloud and Discussing

📖 Deal with your spouse based upon who she is today, not upon what you want her to be. So what if she isn't who she should be today? Are you? Besides, it's not important that she becomes everything you expect. It's important that she becomes like Christ. Your mercy and your strength help carry her there. 📖

📖 Remember that your marriage is *her* call too. She simply has a differing role. Your leadership means allowing her to play her role freely. It doesn't mean you have to be out in front all the time, making all the decisions. *It means allowing the right gifts to surface at the right time in your marriage.* It may mean allowing your wife's gifts to predominate from time to time, especially if you're married to a go-getter like the Proverbs 31 woman. 📖

📖 When I'm eighty-five, I'll be saying, "I'm glad I risked less prestige and achievement in my career for higher achievement in my home." What good is your Christian faith if you can't lay your career on the line in obedience to God's truth? Thousands of martyrs have done far more, and we'll have to look them in the eye someday. I don't want to have to avert my eyes. 📖

Discussion Questions

A. Which parts of these chapters were most helpful or encouraging to you? Why?

B. What is the difference between dealing with your wife as she is and dealing with her as you want her to be? What are the pros and cons of each approach?

C. When has your family leadership squelched your wife's God-given role? When has your leadership enhanced her role and allowed her gifts to surface? Talk about both of these experiences.

D. Together, review the qualities of the Proverbs 31 woman. Imagine being this woman's husband. What areas of family and community life would you feel completely free to leave in her hands? Why?

E. Envision yourself at eighty-five years of age. Can you say: "I'm glad I risked less prestige and achievement in my career for higher achievement in my home"? Why or why not?

F. Talk about a time when you were faced with choosing between your career and your family. What did you do? How did things turn out? What advice do you have for the other men in the group?

igniting your bondservant mind (part A)

This week's reading assignment:

chapters 14–16 in *Every Man's Marriage*

Marital adjustment is simple. Before marriage, you commanded your ship of life based upon the personal convictions and soul essence of one person—you. Now, as skipper of the USS Matrimony, *you must command based upon the convictions and essence of two people. These convictions will sometimes conflict, and it won't be your love that brings oneness out of the impasse, no matter how sincere your emotions. It's your decisions that honor her essence and your actions that bring oneness.*

—from chapter 14 in *Every Man's Marriage*

EVERY MAN's TRUTH
(Your Personal Journey into God's Word)

This is the second half of your look at the Son's example of servanthood. Jesus shows His willingness to extend compassion to the weak and poor and to protect the helpless—all without complaining or needing to draw attention to Himself. As a role model for us, He is beyond compare.

But don't be discouraged. We won't follow Him perfectly. Yet He does call us to take the next small step in this transformation of our attitudes toward our wives. As you read and meditate on these passages, consider what might be the next step for you in moving toward more compassion and less self-centeredness. Ask the Lord to lead you into greater insight and a willingness to take action.

> The Spirit of the Sovereign LORD is on me,
>> because the LORD has anointed me
>> to preach good news to the poor.
> He has sent me to bind up the brokenhearted,
>> to proclaim freedom for the captives
>> and release from darkness for the prisoners,
> to proclaim the year of the LORD's favor
>> and the day of vengeance of our God,
> to comfort all who mourn,
>> and provide for those who grieve in Zion—
> to bestow on them a crown of beauty
>> instead of ashes,
> the oil of gladness
>> instead of mourning,
> and a garment of praise
>> instead of a spirit of despair.
> They will be called oaks of righteousness,
>> a planting of the LORD
>> for the display of his splendor. (Isaiah 61:1-3)

I am the good shepherd; I know my sheep and my sheep know me—just as the Father knows me and I know the Father—and I lay down my life for the sheep.... The reason my Father loves me is that I lay down my life—only to take it up again. No one takes it from me, but I lay it down of my own accord. I have authority to lay it down and authority to take it up again. This command I received from my Father. (John 10:14-15,17-18)

Slaves, submit yourselves to your masters with all respect, not only to those who are good and considerate, but also to those who are harsh. For it is commendable if a man bears up under the pain of unjust suffering because he is conscious of God. But how is it to your credit if you receive a beating for doing wrong and endure it? But if you suffer for doing good and you endure it, this is commendable before God. To this you were called, because Christ suffered for you, leaving you an example, that you should follow in his steps.

> "He committed no sin, and no deceit was found
> in his mouth."

When they hurled their insults at him, he did not retaliate; when he suffered, he made no threats. Instead, he entrusted himself to him who judges justly. He himself bore our sins in his body on the tree, so that we might die to sins and live for righteousness; by his wounds you have been healed. (1 Peter 2:18-24)

1. What forms of compassion do you find in the Anointed One's mission? What connections can you draw to the husband's role in a marriage?

2. Look closely at the "instead of" statements in the Isaiah passage. Think about personal attitudes or actions that you would like to change in your marital relationship. With what would you replace them?

3. Jesus is your Good Shepherd. First, what does this mean to you? Next, consider: What do you think it would mean to your wife to have a good-shepherding husband?

4. As a bondservant ("slave"), how easy or difficult is it to submit to your "master" with all respect? Make this a matter of prayer during the week!

☑ EVERY MAN'S CHOICE
(Questions for Personal Reflection and Examination)

    📖 If our wife is to live fully in marriage, we must study her essence—what she's all about—until we know it like our own. Without such study, our natural male mind-set makes us reckless commanders. We must ignite within ourselves a new mind because reckless commanders sink ships. 📖

📖 Is it fair that our wives set the performance standards when we've already traveled the extra mile and pitched in around the house? Shouldn't she just count her blessings and be thankful for what she has? We need to step inside our wives' Nikes for a moment. Why did they choose these standards in the first place? Because what they view as "the right way" is rooted in their essence. 📖

5. What do you know about your wife's essence so far? How much more do you think is still waiting for you to explore?

6. Do you ever have the feeling of unfairness expressed in the second quote above? When are you most likely to feel resentment toward your wife's performance standards? How do you usually react?

7. When did you last "step into your wife's Nikes"? Think about the good that came from it. Offer a prayer of thanks!

EVERY MAN'S WALK
(Your Guide to Personal Application)

📖 When we're romancing our wives, we have to do what *they* think is fun and what *they* think is romantic. That shows we know them and care for them. Now, if your wife were to romance you, visiting a cookie stand wouldn't cut it at all, but sitting down on a Friday night on the couch with a bowl of popcorn and watching an old Cary Grant movie? Bingo. It's restful, and it's romantic. You're sharing the moment, sharing laughter, and sharing conversation. You're relating to each other, and that builds intimacy. 📖

📖 Don't just *say* you love your wife; reflect that love with your body. It is always easier to talk a good game than to play a good game. Be sure your love is deeper and richer than your words. 📖

8. To what extent do you know what your wife thinks is fun and romantic?

9. Think about a time in your marriage when you talked a good game while not playing a good game. If you could have a second chance in the same situation, what would you do differently?

10. Plan to make a date with your wife this week. Make some notes about what would be fun and romantic—for her. Then take action.

11. In quiet, review what you have written and learned in this week's study. If further thoughts or prayer requests come to your mind and heart, you may want to write them here.

12. a) What for you was the most meaningful concept or truth in this week's study?

b) How would you talk this over with God? Write your response here as a prayer to Him.

c) What do you believe God wants you to do in response to this week's study?

EVERY MAN'S TALK
(Constructive Topics and Questions for Group Discussion)

Key Highlights from the Book for Reading Aloud and Discussing

📖 If we're committed to helping our "master" (our wives) blossom in marriage, we must move beyond a merely logical leadership style. We must seek to be a righteous commander, one who honors her essence always. In other words, we must think sacrificially. Doing so will bring healthy marital adjustment. 📖

📖 Let's get practical and explore sacrificial thinking within the context of a number of marital adjustments we all face.

You'll see how this kind of thinking is far superior to logic in honoring your wife's essence just as you honor your own. 📖

📖 In teaching a young couples' Sunday school class, I challenged the fathers of toddlers to give their wives one night off per week. Several weeks later, I asked whether anyone had begun the practice. Bill proudly raised his hand, but he soon wished he hadn't. After I congratulated him, I turned to his wife, Cindy, and asked how she felt having a night off. 📖

Discussion Questions

A. Which parts of chapters 14 and 15 were most helpful or encouraging to you? Why?

B. How would you describe the differences between a logical leadership style and a sacrificial leadership style? If possible, offer some practical illustrations from your experience.

C. Together, review the four marital adjustments discussed in chapter 14 under the heading, "Is It Everything She Wants?" Analyze and critique the authors' views related to each situation. Do you agree or disagree with their perspective? Why? What is your experience in these areas?

D. Recall the story of Bill and Cindy in chapter 15. Why was Cindy unhappy with her so-called break? Do you tend to side with Bill or Cindy in this situation? What practical advice would you offer to each partner?

For a twelve-week study,
save the following material for next week.

☑ EVERY MAN'S CHOICE
(Questions for Personal Reflection and Examination)

📖 I can truly imagine that a bondservant who loved his master not only served, but he served with a light heart. He knew he was helping the master he loved. He loved to see his master's face brighten when he entered his presence. He lived for the moments when his master said, "My dear brother, I don't know what I would do without you." 📖

📖 If the passion's not there in your marriage, you won't find much oneness. Sure, you're comfortable with your wife, and she's the best friend you have. As a mother, you may think she's matchless. She may still knock your socks off when she slips into a sundress.… But such sentiments don't reveal that you've necessarily done anything more than love *you* in the marriage. Both your passion for oneness and your passion for serving show that you love *her*. It brings joy to *her* journey. 📖

13. Are you able to serve your wife with a light heart? Why, or why not?

14. Consider the level of passion in your marriage. How can you tell that it is contributing to oneness? How is your lack of passion hindering the oneness in your marriage?

15. What do the authors mean when they say that you are only loving you when passion is based on sentiment alone? In practical terms, what more is needed?

📖 EVERY MAN'S WALK

(Your Guide to Personal Application)

    📖 I sucked it up and helped Brenda as much as humanly possible. Problem is, I wore my service like a badge, practically demanding trumpet blasts and salutes from Brenda. As I recall, the Medal of Honor wasn't forthcoming. 📖

    📖 When I'm gone, I want Brenda to miss our prayers. I want her to miss our laughter. I want her to find no secrets where I had compromised her values in private. I want her to miss our bedtimes and to miss the person who defended her soul. I want her certain that her married years were the happiest years of her life, not the loneliest. I want her to enjoy this journey, and I will give my life away before it's taken. 📖

16. Think of the specific times and situations when you are tempted to wear your service like a badge. Choose one of these times and ask yourself: *How can I take this badge off the next time I enter a similar situation?*

17. How badly would your wife miss you if you were to die tomorrow? Ask her, and compare answers.

18. What would it mean, in practical terms, for you to defend your wife's soul? How do you plan to do this in the days ahead?

19. In quiet, review what you have written and learned in this week's study. If further thoughts or prayer requests come to your mind and heart, you may want to write them here.

20. a) What for you was the most meaningful concept or truth in this week's study?

    b) How would you talk this over with God? Write your response here as a prayer to Him.

c) What do you believe God wants you to do in response to this
week's study?

👤👤 EVERY MAN'S TALK
(Constructive Topics and Questions for Group Discussion)

Key Highlights from the Book for Reading Aloud and Discussing

📖 Imagine that God offered you the two options below.
Which would you choose?

Option 1: Working twelve hours a day for two years in the
business of your dreams, a commitment that would quadruple your income.

Option 2: Working twelve hours a day for two years to
passionately live out a bondservant's heart when you're at
home, an effort that would quadruple your wife's joy.

📖 I took the fork to Moline.... When I rolled into Moline
around 1:30 A.M., I was beat, and the kids were crabby.
Brenda...stumbled out into the living room and into my
arms sighing, "Oh, I've missed you. It's so good to have you
back." How I live for these moments! Would I do it again?
Oh, yeah!

This is every woman's desire. *You can settle for mediocrity,
or you can pay the price for something great.* If you pay the
price and meet the terms, a deep intimacy will overflow your
lives together. 📖

Discussion Questions

E. Which parts of chapter 16 were most helpful or encouraging to you? Why?

F. Which of the two options in the first quote above would you choose? Talk about your reasons.

G. Recall the story of Fred's fork in the road. Do you agree with his decision to go to Moline? Honestly, what do you think you would have done in the same situation? Why?

H. Tell a story about a fork in the road you've faced in your marriage. Talk about what you decided—and what you learned.

I. Close your session by asking a volunteer to read aloud the letter in which Myrtle Dobson speaks of her husband's death. Ask for reactions to the letter before you take prayer requests from each participant.

igniting your bondservant mind (part B)

This week's reading assignment:

chapters 17-19 in *Every Man's Marriage*

The bondservant once stood on the auction block of shame because of his own fool-ishness and sin. By grace, his master lovingly restored the tattered pieces of his life. Now the bondservant hates sin, especially his own, but when it affects the master who gave up so much for him, he hates it even more. He knows his master has every right to inspect him and confront him, for his sin affects the strength of his master's house and all who live there.

—from chapter 19 in *Every Man's Marriage*

EVERY MAN'S TRUTH
(Your Personal Journey into God's Word)

Before you begin this study, read and meditate upon the Bible passages below during a personal quiet time. These scriptures deal with the Holy Spirit's presence and leading in your life. If your mind is to be transformed for God's glory, then the Spirit must be the motivating force behind this change. He alone has the power to produce ongoing spiritual renewal within you and within your marriage. Thankfully, He wants to do it! Are you open to the Spirit's guidance today?

> And I will ask the Father, and he will give you another Counselor to be with you forever—the Spirit of truth. The world cannot accept him, because it neither sees him nor knows him. But you know him, for he lives with you and will be in you. (John 14:16-17)

> Those who live according to the sinful nature have their minds set on what that nature desires; but those who live in accordance with the Spirit have their minds set on what the Spirit desires. The mind of sinful man is death, but the mind controlled by the Spirit is life and peace; the sinful mind is hostile to God. It does not submit to God's law, nor can it do so. Those controlled by the sinful nature cannot please God.
> You, however, are controlled not by the sinful nature but by the Spirit, if the Spirit of God lives in you. And if anyone does not have the Spirit of Christ, he does not belong to Christ. (Romans 8:5-9)

> No one knows the thoughts of God except the Spirit of God. We have not received the spirit of the world but the Spirit who is from God, that we may understand what God has freely given us. This is what we speak, not in words taught us by human wisdom but in words taught by the Spirit, expressing spiritual truths in spiritual words. The man without the Spirit does not accept the things that come from the Spirit of God, for they are foolishness to him, and he cannot

understand them, because they are spiritually discerned. The spiritual man makes judgments about all things, but he himself is not subject to any man's judgment:

> "For who has known the mind of the Lord
> that he may instruct him?"

But we have the mind of Christ. (1 Corinthians 2:11-16)

1. Where is the Holy Spirit right now? How often do you consult this heavenly Counselor about your everyday life?

2. Where is your mind normally "set" or focused? Why? Suppose you were to ask more regularly during your day: "What do You desire, Holy Spirit?"

3. What are the most precious spiritual truths that you have been led by the Spirit to understand?

4. How can you let what you understand of the spiritual life seep into your heart and actions?

☑ EVERY MAN'S CHOICE

(Questions for Personal Reflection and Examination)

📖 Submitting your character to Scripture builds your wife's trust in you. This trust will return mercy to you. She'll give you the benefit of the doubt whenever your leadership is shaky.... After my (Steve) relationship with Sandy began to improve, we felt free to talk about the days when our marriage was anything but a marriage. She told me that through the tough times she was always hopeful for a great future together because of one thing: She knew I was up early reading Scripture and having a quiet time. 📖

📖 Raising kids is teamwork. Give up your individual rights and the blatant exertion of authority and be your wife's teammate. Help her. Share duties. Pitch in. Never undermine your wife's position by making yourself look more important. Help your children learn to honor her as their mother and to appreciate the value of a woman. This bedrock principle will have a tremendous impact on your kids' futures, especially their marriages. 📖

5. How did Sandy's statement to Steve (in the first quote above) make you feel? What is your reaction to the idea that your Scripture-submitted character builds trust within your wife?

6. What is the level of teamwork in your home when it comes to caring for the children? Are you convinced of the importance of working closely on this with your wife?

Every Man's WALK
(Your Guide to Personal Application)

How does a husband go about leading spiritually, like Christ, in his home? You start by taking these six steps in your life.

Men often feel they have the authority to make these child-rearing decisions alone. We don't. The terms of oneness must constrain our rights. Listen to Susie.

7. Review the six steps for spiritual leadership outlined in chapter 17. Apply them to your life by analyzing where you are in each step. Make

a list of (a) praises for the things you are doing well, and (b) prayer requests for areas that seem to need improvement.

8. Review Susie and Rick's story in chapter 18 regarding child rearing—and Rick's letting the kids watch *Rambo* and *Die Hard*. If you were a marriage counselor, how would you likely approach this problem with the couple? What personal application can you draw from their experience?

9. In quiet, review what you have written and learned in this week's study. If further thoughts or prayer requests come to your mind and heart, you may want to write them here.

10. a) What for you was the most meaningful concept or truth in this week's study?

b) How would you talk this over with God? Write your response here as a prayer to Him.

c) What do you believe God wants you to do in response to this week's study?

👥 EVERY MAN'S TALK
(Constructive Topics and Questions for Group Discussion)

Key Highlights from the Book for Reading Aloud and Discussing

> 📖 Jill said, "Allen is much quicker to submit to Scripture than I am. He's quick to fix anything in his life that he feels doesn't line up with Scripture. He has always been submissive to God's ways, and this makes me trust him and feel one with him." Again, note the security this submission to Scripture brings to your realm. On the other hand, failing to deal with sin brings disorder, confusion, and fear. It tramples your wife's convictions and puts a stumbling block in the pathway of oneness. 📖

📖 No one in the family should be quicker to forgive than you. Forgiveness is the cornerstone of Christianity. It doesn't come naturally to me, however. I prefer a less subtle policy of Mutually Assured Destruction! If someone launches ten missiles at me, in retaliation, I'll launch thirty just for good measure. Mercy? Forget it! I'd rather hang you on the wall until dawn. If you're like me, we needn't remain this way. Hebrews 5:1-2 says, "Every high priest…is able to deal gently with those who are ignorant and are going astray, since he himself is subject to weakness." 📖

📖 There's no area [for example, child rearing] where you'll feel more justified in ignoring your wife or in being less sensitive to her essence. This position is dangerous because, when it comes to deciding how to raise the children, playing Chief Tiebreaker at the wrong time can cripple oneness more severely than anything else can. 📖

Discussion Questions

A. Which parts of these chapters were most helpful or encouraging to you? Why?

B. Allen seems like a saint. In your opinion, how realistic is it to think that any guy can quickly submit to Scripture when he sees an area of sin in his life? If you can, share a personal experience about this.

C. How quickly do you forgive? What tends to hold you back? What works to move you forward?

D. Why do men typically want to play Chief Tiebreaker when it comes to child-rearing decisions? According to the authors, what is a better way?

E. Steve said that he never had a secret with his daughter that he told her not to share with her mother. What is the effect of a stance like that? Where, in your marriage, could you apply a similar principle (of not placing the kids between you and your wife)?

For a twelve-week study,
save the following material for next week.

☑ EVERY MAN'S CHOICE
(Questions for Personal Reflection and Examination)

📖 As spiritual leader in your home, what's your attitude toward your position? Countless men think their title of spiritual leader places them above scrutiny, and they refuse any kind of confrontation by their wives. Contrast this with the bondservant's attitude.… Does your wife have the right to question you about your actions? Or are you above question? 📖

📖 While it is *technically* impossible for your wife to change you, let us also remind you of something. When it comes to sinful, trampling behaviors, it is flat-out unbiblical for a husband to declare, "My wife has no right to try to change me." It's more accurate to say, "I married my mate, for better or worse, and she traded her freedoms to marry me. I have a responsibility before God and my wife to be conformed to Christ. I will not rest until my sins are under control. I won't be a quitter, and I won't dog it." 📖

11. When was the last time your wife confronted you about a mistake, shortcoming, or sin in your life? How did you respond? Why?

12. Can you make the following pledge: "I won't rest until my sins are under control"? What, for you, will be the most difficult aspect of keeping such a commitment?

👟 EVERY MAN'S WALK
(Your Guide to Personal Application)

📖 I (Steve) discovered a damaging sin that I was reluctant to give up. It was the sin of nondisclosure. I kept a private little world in my head where fantasy reigned and "what ifs" and "if onlys" ruled. I wasn't on the Internet because I didn't need to be. I had enough downloaded images in my mind to last a lifetime. While sitting in a counselor's office one time, I was confronted with my dishonesty. No, I didn't come out

and tell blatant lies, but I lived a lie by not telling the whole
story or by conveniently leaving out details I should have
shared. 📖

📖 And when the power of sin is working in us, what is
Christ's advice for us? Tell our wives to shut up? Cross our
arms defiantly over our hardened hearts to protect them any-
time someone comes near? Tell our wives to get used to it
and to join us in covering it all up...for the sake of the kids?

Hardly. Here's God's advice: "Be earnest, and repent"
(Revelation 3:19). 📖

13. What is your reaction to the idea of "the sin of nondisclosure"? How
do you see this operating in your life?

14. Name some key areas of required repentance in your life. How will
you approach your wife about this in order to open up your heart to
her? Make a plan!

15. In quiet, review what you have written and learned in this week's study. If further thoughts or prayer requests come to your mind and heart, you may want to write them here.

16. a) What for you was the most meaningful concept or truth in this week's study?

b) How would you talk this over with God? Write your response here as a prayer to Him.

c) What do you believe God wants you to do in response to this week's study?

EVERY MAN'S TALK

(Constructive Topics and Questions for Group Discussion)

Key Highlights from the Book for Reading Aloud and Discussing

The responsibility for holding each other accountable must be especially true in marriage, since the consequences of sin immediately affect the other partner. We're one flesh, so our sin in effect becomes her sin! Yet as leaders in our homes, we often refuse scrutiny.

We love that important seat of leadership in the home, but we—like Brant—deflect scrutiny like the finest Pharisee. Amy told us of her recent discovery that Brant, her husband of twenty-four years, had visited pornographic Web sites. The news devastated her.... Now there's a very thick wall between them.

When Sandy has something she wants me (Steve) to work on, she always starts by saying, "Now I just want to be sure you want to be told about a problem I might be seeing."

"Sure," I reply, but then I start repeating over and over in my head, "Don't be defensive. Don't be defensive." By giving Sandy the chance to "improve" me, I've eliminated some bad habits and even forfeited some Texan slang. I'm better for what she does for me.

Discussion Questions

F. Which parts of these chapters were most helpful or encouraging
to you? Why?

G. Do you agree that your sin, in effect, becomes your wife's sin? How
were you affected upon first encountering this idea in the text?

H. Review the story of Brant and Amy in chapter 19. To what extent can
you relate to Amy's reaction to her husband? If you were Brant's best
friend, how would you advise him?

I. Can you relate to Steve's technique of repeating, "Don't be defensive"?
How hard or easy is it for you to keep defensiveness under control
when your wife is pointing out a fault? What usually happens at those
times? What would you like to happen in the future?

J. Look again at chapter 19's four paths you can take to make
needed changes. Which one are you most likely to choose in
the year ahead? Why?

K. As a group, make the responses to *J* a matter of prayer.

enjoying a resurrected relationship (part A)

This week's reading assignment:

chapters 20-21 in *Every Man's Marriage*

Most Christian couples pray their hearts out before marriage, believing God has brought them together. We expect our "unique" love to guarantee marital oneness. Because of that, we confidently stride into marriage, expecting our sexual fantasies to be fulfilled and possibly exceeded simply because we deeply love one another. We expect sex to be so good our wives will want everything our hearts and minds desire in the marriage bed.

—from chapter 20 in *Every Man's Marriage*

EVERY MAN'S TRUTH
(Your Personal Journey into God's Word)

Read and meditate upon the Bible passages below, which deal with God's gift of sexuality. Focus on thankfulness for your own body and how wonderfully it is made. Give thanks for the sexual desire God has placed within you, which can lead you into a deeper intimacy with your wife. Also offer praise to God that one day, when we reach the heavenly kingdom, He will fully satisfy all our earthly longings (of which sexual desire is only a part).

> God created man in his own image,
>> in the image of God he created him;
>> male and female he created them.
>>> (Genesis 1:27)

> May your fountain be blessed,
>> and may you rejoice in the wife of your youth.
> A loving doe, a graceful deer—
>> may her breasts satisfy you always,
>> may you ever be captivated by her love.
>>> (Proverbs 5:18-19)

> Enjoy life with your wife, whom you love, all the days of this meaningless life that God has given you under the sun. (Ecclesiastes 9:9)

> Marriage should be honored by all, and the marriage bed kept pure, for God will judge the adulterer and all the sexually immoral. (Hebrew 13:4)

1. God created the sexes—and sex. What does this tell you about the God whom you love and worship?

2. According to the Proverbs passage, marital sex can be a great blessing. What attitudes help make it so? From your experience, what things tend to hinder this blessing, so that you become less "captivated by her love"?

3. God seems to delight in giving us the joy of sex in marriage. He honors marriage and the marriage bed. So why is there often so much shame surrounding the issues of sexuality? What forms of healing do we Christians need in this area? What about our society at large?

☑ EVERY MAN'S CHOICE
(Questions for Personal Reflection and Examination)

> 📖 In premarriage class, Brenda and I always circle the room asking, "What do you hope to get out of marriage that you couldn't get if you remained single?" The answers should give every man an inkling of what's coming just around the bend in his new marriage. Most men begin by speaking loftily about companionship and working on dreams together. The more honest ones cite sex as a great reason to get hitched. In the twelve years of leading these

classes, we can't ever remember a woman answering this way, yet many guys anticipate their wives being as excited about sex as they are. 📖

📖 When we put these three differences together, it can stretch our credibility with our wives: "Oh, so you really feel love for me tonight and you really want to make love, huh? Well, what do you know? It's been seventy-two hours since our last go at it. Hmmm. It doesn't sound much like love to me. Sounds more like some kind of hormone bath! Go fly a kite!" 📖

4. Why do you think future brides tend not to list sex as a prime reason to get married? What point does this bring home to you about how a husband can best pursue sexual oneness in marriage?

5. How do the three big differences between men and women contribute to the kind of statement made by a wife in the quote above? When have you heard something similar from your own wife? What can you do to help remedy the situation?

👟 EVERY MAN'S WALK
(Your Guide to Personal Application)

📖 With precision, Jesus says, "I ask a lot from wives in marriage, but submitting sexually is one of the most difficult of all. Have you made it easy for her to help you in this way? My friend, look to the log in your own eye before you point a finger at your cherished one." 📖

📖 Because of our differences, wives typically won't be in the mood as often as their husbands. How do we get their engines to turn over even when they aren't in the mood?... We husbands have to at least be sexually attractive. And this phrase probably means exactly the opposite of what you're thinking. A woman's sexual attraction to a man is based on relationship, not sight. *One thing that always makes you sexually desirable to her is oneness.* 📖

6. What things can you do to help make it easy for your wife to submit sexually?

7. According to the authors, what does it mean to be sexually attractive to a wife? Rate yourself for sexual attractiveness. How could you improve?

8. Do you agree that oneness is sexually attractive to your wife? When could you take some time to discuss this with her?

9. In quiet, review what you have written and learned in this week's study. If further thoughts or prayer requests come to your mind and heart, you may want to write them here.

10. a) What for you was the most meaningful concept or truth in this week's study?

b) How would you talk this over with God? Write your response here as a prayer to Him.

c) What do you believe God wants you to do in response to this week's study?

👥 EVERY MAN'S TALK
(Constructive Topics and Questions for Group Discussion)

Key Highlights from the Book for Reading Aloud and Discussing

> 📖 Singles can't understand, but married men can. While most married men expect sexual oneness to be a slam dunk, it's more like a half-court shot. Sexual incompatibility is as common as two-week paydays. Mark said, "I don't want to seem like a sex addict or anything, but I probably have as many unmet sexual desires now as I did before marriage." 📖

📖 *Why are so many otherwise godly women sinning against their husbands this way?* Sex is as natural as breathing, so it isn't natural for them to withdraw this way. Why is sexual submission so hard for our wives? For one reason, it's because we're poor spiritual leaders, but it's also hard because they aren't like us. Let's briefly consider three of the most significant differences. 📖

Discussion Questions

A. Which parts of these chapters were most helpful or encouraging to you? Why?

B. Ask volunteers to react to the first quote above, about unmet sexual desires after marriage. Why is this hard for singles to understand?

C. Together, review the three significant differences between men's and women's sexuality discussed in chapter 20. Without revealing personal marital details, talk about how men can work at overcoming the obstacles these differences put in the pathway toward intimacy.

D. Recall Steve's story about wanting to hold hands with Sandy before they were married. Steve found later that Sandy wasn't much interested in sex, either! What was his solution? Do you agree that his approach could be effective for most men in a similar situation? Talk about it.

E. Briefly review the letter from Raymond in chapter 20. He asks: "I'm wondering if you have any advice for me." What would your advice be?

For a twelve-week study,
save the following material for next week.

☑ Every Man's CHOICE
(Questions for Personal Reflection and Examination)

📖 Sexual oneness is no different than other kinds of oneness. It has terms as well. Comply with the terms, and sexual oneness lives. Ignore those terms, and it dies. We need to act righteously in the marriage bed. If we do, the right feelings follow. 📖

📖 The simple magnetism of love and physical attraction won't build the emotional and spiritual communion necessary for a satisfactory sex life. Mutual submission will, however: "The wife's body does not belong to her alone but also to her husband. In the same way, the husband's body does not belong to him alone but also to his wife" (1 Corinthians 7:4).

You can't mistake it: Mutual submission is embedded in this verse. God expects mutual submission to be perfected in the marriage bed. 📖

11. What are the terms of sexual oneness to which the authors refer? Which are you ignoring?

12. Why are physical magnetism and emotion insufficient bases for building sexual oneness?

13. What does it mean to you to experience mutual submission in the marriage bed?

📖 EVERY MAN'S WALK
(Your Guide to Personal Application)

 📖 "Unromantic" obedience has its place in the marriage bed. You needn't start with the right feelings. The right feelings will always follow right actions. If we plan to love our wife as we love ourselves, we must make room for her essence, and that has nothing to do with emotions. As we pointed out in the previous chapter, attaining sexual oneness calls for personal sacrifice. And you either sacrifice for her essence, or you don't. 📖

📖 Have you wondered why your sex life isn't more satisfying? You've noticed that there's an empty spot. To fill it, you've asked for more variety, more frequency, and more foldouts on the headboard. But what you really need is the emotional and spiritual communion that comes with sexual oneness. Consider the e-mail from a reader of *Every Man's Battle,* a guy we'll call Matt. 📖

14. Do you agree that there is a place for "unromantic" obedience in the marriage bed? Have you talked about this with your wife? What kinds of sacrifice would this kind of obedience require?

15. Look again at the e-mail from Matt. Can you believe this guy—that he would never trade, for circuit-breaking sex, the pure communion he has now with his wife? To what extent is this e-mail a motivator for you to pursue sexual oneness with your wife? What next step do you need to take?

16. In quiet, review what you have written and learned in this week's study. If further thoughts or prayer requests come to your mind and heart, you may want to write them here.

17. a) What for you was the most meaningful concept or truth in this week's study?

    b) How would you talk this over with God? Write your response here as a prayer to Him.

    c) What do you believe God wants you to do in response to this week's study?

👓👤 EVERY MAN'S TALK

(Constructive Topics and Questions for Group Discussion)

Key Highlights from the Book for Reading Aloud and Discussing

📖 Was God surprised the first time He heard a wife rudely compare her husband to a dog in heat? Nope. Did He think it amusing? Not at all, because He knew that soon thereafter she'd begin to withdraw sexually without realizing that this withers her husband in the exact same way he withers her with his silence. 📖

📖 Whether we like it or not, there's a distinct place for male submission in the marriage bed. Chances are we may not like it because no sacrifice seems more costly than sexual sacrifice. It's one thing to submit to her essence and to let her buy the more expensive washing machine. It's quite another to allow her sexual essence to set the terms of oneness and define our sexual fulfillment. 📖

Discussion Questions

F. Which parts of these chapters were most helpful or encouraging to you? Why?

G. The authors speak of the wife's setting the terms for sexual oneness in a marriage. What are those terms in your marriage?

H. How would it feel to be compared to a dog in heat? Do you agree that this is how your wife feels when her needs for oneness are ignored?

I. Is it truly reasonable to think that a man could allow his wife's sexual essence to set the terms of his sexual fulfillment? Think about it! What does this challenge say about the degree of difficulty of sexual sacrifice? (Note: You may wish to refer to the story of Richard in chapter 21 and earlier.)

J. The authors state that, for our wives, sex with us should be "as pure as prayer." In practical terms, what does this mean to you? What attitudes and actions can help this come to fruition in any man's marriage?

enjoying a resurrected relationship (part B)

This week's reading assignment:

chapters 22–24 in *Every Man's Marriage*

Most of us men have no idea what marriage should look like, and our clumsy efforts to be a "good husband" reflect it. And when it comes to "male leadership," many of us "lead" simply by "taking charge." As you've seen in this book, grabbing the reins didn't work too well for me.... Now, in closing, I want to express once more God's plan for good marital leadership, but this time reduce it to a single verse: "Submit to one another out of reverence for Christ" (Ephesians 5:21).

This is God's simple plan for oneness in marriage. May you follow it, and may your marriage be forever changed.

—from chapter 24 in *Every Man's Marriage*

EVERY MAN'S TRUTH
(Your Personal Journey into God's Word)

As you begin your final study in this workbook, review again in your mind's eye what you would like your marriage to be. Then read and meditate upon the following scripture passages, which deal with God's plan for your marriage. Consider how your vision and God's vision compare and contrast. As you immerse yourself in God's Word, prayerfully open your heart to Him with your hopes and dreams for enjoying a resurrected relationship with your wife.

> The LORD God said, "It is not good for the man to be alone.
> I will make a helper suitable for him." (Genesis 2:18)

> But a man who commits adultery lacks judgment;
> > whoever does so destroys himself.
> Blows and disgrace are his lot,
> > and his shame will never be wiped away;
> for jealousy arouses a husband's fury,
> > and he will show no mercy when he takes revenge.
> He will not accept any compensation;
> > he will refuse the bribe, however great it is.
> > > (Proverbs 6:32-35)

> Another thing you do: You flood the LORD's altar with tears.
> You weep and wail because he no longer pays attention to
> your offerings or accepts them with pleasure from your
> hands. You ask, "Why?" It is because the LORD is acting as
> the witness between you and the wife of your youth, because
> you have broken faith with her, though she is your partner,
> the wife of your marriage covenant.
> Has not the LORD made them one? In flesh and spirit
> they are his. And why one? Because he was seeking godly off-
> spring. So guard yourself in your spirit, and do not break
> faith with the wife of your youth. (Malachi 2:13-15)

Submit to one another out of reverence for Christ.

Wives, submit to your husbands as to the Lord....

Husbands, love your wives, just as Christ loved the church
and gave himself up for her to make her holy.... In this same
way, husbands ought to love their wives as their own bodies.
He who loves his wife loves himself. (Ephesians 5:21-22,25-
26,28)

1. In light of Genesis 2:18, how is marriage an act of God's compassion
   toward us?

2. Besides the obvious grievous consequences, name some other reasons
   why adultery and divorce are so wrong.

3. How do you handle temptations to "break faith" with the wife of your
   youth?

4. How, in terms of actual results, is loving your wife like loving yourself?

☑ EVERY MAN'S CHOICE

(Questions for Personal Reflection and Examination)

📖 Personal convictions will result in impasses between believers, including husbands and wives, but such disagreements needn't break unity. So how do we overcome impasses lovingly? As we said earlier, traditionally the leader calls for a vote and breaks any ties in his favor. As you recall, that's not what Paul says a Christian leader should do (see Romans 14:13-15,19-21).... When it comes to sex in marriage, you must be a leader with a soft heart, a man who can submit his own rights for the sake of oneness. 📖

📖 As with the other areas of marriage, you need to study your wife's sexual essence. 📖

5. How do you tend to break through the impasses with your wife?

6. Take a moment to read Romans 14:13-23 in your favorite translation. Do you believe the principles here can translate to a husband and wife's disagreements about sex? If so, how does this passage apply to your marital relationship?

7. To what extent have you studied your wife's sexual essence as defined by the authors? What have you learned? How has your learning challenged you to grow in sacrificial love?

📖 EVERY MAN'S WALK
(Your Guide to Personal Application)

📖 Looking at this chart [see page 267] with sets and subsets, do you feel as though you're back in school? Well, I needed to be sent to school, and I was willing to let God be my teacher. Through this diagram, God conveyed four principles for me to follow if I was going to honor Brenda's convictions and sexual essence always. 📖

📖 The area labeled *B* is off-limits forever to the husband and must never be brought up again. 📖

8. Review the ABC chart of sexual practices presented in chapter 22. Are you able to live by the four rules the authors suggest? When could you talk these over with your wife?

9. How difficult is it for you to accept the statement in the second quote above?

10. If your anger about this "off-limits forever" rule seems to be escalating, will you consider counseling? What about bringing the matter to God in prayer—regularly—in the weeks and months ahead?

11. In quiet, review what you have written and learned in this week's study. If further thoughts or prayer requests come to your mind and heart, you may want to write them here.

12. a) What for you was the most meaningful concept or truth in this week's study?

b) How would you talk this over with God? Write your response here as a prayer to Him.

c) What do you believe God wants you to do in response to this week's study?

🙂🙂 EVERY MAN'S **TALK**
(Constructive Topics and Questions for Group Discussion)

Key Highlights from the Book for Reading Aloud and Discussing

📖 Paul understood that pressing his rights at the expense of God's purposes would be wrong, so he wouldn't sin against God by eating meat and causing a brother to stumble. Following this principle will be especially important in the sexual realm because everything is so personal there. When it comes to sex in marriage, you must be a leader with a soft heart, a man who can submit his own rights for the sake of oneness. 📖

📖 When I was in second grade, a lunchroom rule forced us to eat something from every serving of food on our plates. I have a stomach of steel, so this caused no problem until one fateful spring day. On my tray that day was a dry white biscuit glopped with smelly white gravy and thin slices of reddish "meat." It gagged me to look at it, and it gagged me to sniff it. 📖

📖 Imagine your own daughter coming to you in tears after a few months of marriage, crying because her husband forces her to have sex with handcuffs on. It hurts her wrists physically, and it demeans her to the core of her soul. Would your relationship with your son-in-law remain unaffected? Mine wouldn't. When you dishonor your wife's sexual essence, God is just as ticked as you would be with that son-in-law, and He isn't smiling upon your marriage bed. 📖

Discussion Questions

A. Which parts of these chapters were most helpful or encouraging to you? Why?

B. Review Romans 14 and think about the apostle Paul's method of solving disputes among Christians. Why would it be so difficult to apply these principles to the disagreements between a man and a wife about what is "appropriate" sexually? That is, can you, personally, submit your own rights for the sake of oneness in this area?

C. Talk about Fred's second-grade experience with gagging. Ever been there? In your opinion, is this a good analogy or a bad one? What is the point that comes through to you?

D. Talk together about exactly what it means to dishonor a wife's sexual essence. Consider how men can begin reversing the damage they may have already done in a marriage because of this.

E. One man asked: "But how can cutting back on variety improve my sexual fulfillment?" Summarize how the authors answered him. What is your answer?

F. Briefly skim the letter from Brenda Stoeker at the end of the book. What statements or ideas struck a particular chord with you? Talk about it. Then spend some time praying for one another before ending your study. (Consider having a follow-up meeting in the future. Perhaps you could plan a get-together for fellowship and briefly share about the practical impact of this study.)

don't keep it to yourself

If you've just completed the *Every Man's Marriage Workbook* on your own and you found it to be a helpful and valuable experience, we encourage you to consider organizing a group of men and helping lead them through the book and workbook together.

You'll find more information about starting such a group in the section titled "Questions You May Have About This Workbook."

Steve can be reached by e-mail at sarterburn@newlife.com.

Fred can be reached by e-mail at fred@stoekergroup.com
or at www.fredstoeker.com.

---

every man's battle
workshops

from New Life Ministries

new Life Ministries receives hundreds of calls every month from Christian men who are struggling to stay pure in the midst of daily challenges to their sexual integrity and from pastors who are looking for guidance in how to keep fragile marriages from falling apart all around them.

As part of our commitment to equip individuals to win these battles, New Life Ministries has developed biblically based workshops directly geared to answer these needs. These workshops are held several times per year around the country.

- Our workshops **for men** are structured to equip men with the tools necessary to maintain sexual integrity and enjoy healthy, productive relationships.

- Our workshops **for church leaders** are targeted to help pastors and men's ministry leaders develop programs to help families being attacked by this destructive addiction.

Some comments from previous workshop attendees:

"An awesome, life-changing experience. Awesome teaching, teacher, content and program." —DAVE

"God has truly worked a great work in me since the EMB workshop. I am fully confident that with God's help, I will be restored in my ministry position. Thank you for your concern. I realize that this is a battle, but I now have the weapons of warfare as mentioned in Ephesians 6:10, and I am using them to gain victory!" —KEN

"It's great to have a workshop you can confidently recommend to anyone without hesitation, knowing that it is truly life changing. Your labors are not in vain!" —DR. BRAD STENBERG, Pasadena, CA

If sexual temptation is threatening your marriage or your church, please call **1-800-NEW-LIFE** to speak with one of our specialists.

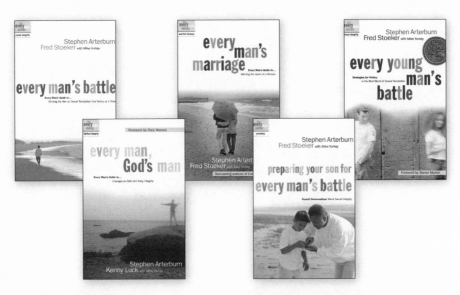